Harnessing the Power of Tension

A paradoxical approach to building alliances at home, in the boardroom, on campus and in communities

Brenda Naomi Rosenberg

Samia Moustapha Bahsoun

Tectonic Leadership Center

For more information and further discussion, visit

http://tectonicleadership.org

ISBN: 978-1-942011-12-5

Version 1.0

Cover art by Cody Harrell

Cover photo and interior photos by Brenda Naomi Rosenberg

Published By

Tectonic Leadership Center

For information about customized editions, bulk purchases or permissions, contact the Tectonic Leadership Center at brenda@tectonicleadership.org.

Contents

Dedication

Our sincere thanks to Sandra Seligman, our dear friend and "book angel" who supports our work and this publication with both love and funding.

Acknowledgements

Only an idea in a state of alert is capable of evolution.

Etienne Klein, from the book *Conversation With a Sphynx*

To our husbands: Howard Rosenberg and George Melton, for their endless patience and for learning with us that tension is an opportunity in our marriages.

To our departed mothers: Amira Bahsoun and Bella Cohen, who loved us despite the tension we caused them from inception.

To our fathers: Herbert Cohen, in blessed memory, for teaching Brenda how to see the beauty in the world through the lens of her camera; and Moustapha Bahsoun, for his wisdom and for introducing Samia to paradoxical thinking.

In memory of Debbie Ford, our friend and teacher, who introduced us and believed that, together, we can change the world by bringing our communities out of the shadows.

The Path to Self-Destruction

Fear is the main source of superstition, and one of the main sources of cruelty. To conquer fear is the beginning of wisdom.

Bertrand Russell

The world is indeed in emotional **High Red Alert.**

From the Red Sea to the Mississippi, headlines read: "Fear mixes with anger as Ferguson braces for more unrest," "Holocaust fears haunt Israelis as they prepare for possible war," "Colorado girls' effort to join ISIS stokes fear in Muslim community," "Fear and violence in transgender Baltimore: 'It's scary trusting anyone.'"

The Southern Poverty Law Center (SPLC), a prominent civil rights organization based in Montgomery, AL indicated in a 2012 study that—despite the recent decline in the number of hate groups from 2013—"there are still enormous numbers of radical groups operating ... more than 2,000 of them, including hate and Patriot organizations." Another report stated that there were just 602 of these groups nationally in 2000. According to the SLPC report:

> *The single most important factor that has driven the growth of the radical right over the last five years, the ongoing demographic change to a non-white majority over the course of the next three decades, is still a source of enormous angst and rage for many. And the fact that the Tea Parties and the far right of the Republican Party have lost some of their public support does not mean that millions of Americans do not still sympathize. A shocking poll by Fairleigh Dickinson University's PublicMind last spring showed that 29% of Americans think that armed rebellion may soon be necessary.*

Today, the world is afraid of Muslims and their motives. Sixty years ago, Hitler used fear to rally half a continent against Jews, engineering their total elimination. Fear continues to be the weapon of choice in small and large conflicts worldwide as world leaders play on each other's physiological responses to such fear. Originally discovered by the great Harvard physiologist Walter Cannon, this physiological response known as "fight or flight" is hardwired into the human brain. It represents a genetic wisdom designed to protect from bodily harm. Leaders and their constituents have been indoctrinated to believe that these are the only responses to fear. In fact, such conditioning is so prevalent that it is rarely questioned when leaders use fear mongering for their own personal ambitions and act as protectors for their constituents.

As the fight or flight response fuels tension and fear generated by mistrust, lack of respect, unmet expectations, denial of identity and targeted aggression, someone must harness the power of tension to inform the other and deconstruct the negative narratives that surround each other. Then, the attention is put on creating new solutions together that benefit both groups.

Conflict surprises like a tsunami. With little warning, a wave of astronomical proportion hits shores, engulfs cities, shatters communities and disrupts lives. There is just enough time to gasp some air until another wave forms and blasts the worlds' shores again and again.

Currently, the U.S. Congress is experiencing a similar historical rift. They are polarizing constituents on every issue from the nuclear talks with Iran to the conflict between law enforcement and the black community—even immigration reform.

In these times of intense pressure and constant turbulence, in the face of perceived powerlessness, what will it take to shake up resigned minds? How can the world's leaders prevent bullying, homophobia, racism? Who can solve the prevalence of genocide?

 **TECTONIC LEADERSHIP EXERCISE**

Do you remember a time in your life when you avoided tension?

Describe the situation.
What was the outcome?
Did you wish for a different outcome? Describe.

_____

_____

_____

_____

_____

_____

_____

_____

_____

_____

TECTONIC LEADERSHIP EXERCISE

What is a situation of tension you would like to transform?

Describe the situation.

_____

_____

_____

_____

_____

_____

_____

_____

_____

_____

Harnessing the Power of Tension

Our mind is capable of passing beyond the dividing line we have drawn for it. Beyond the pairs of opposites of which the world consists, other, new insights begin.

Hermann Hesse

What if people could harness the power of tension? What if people could use tension instead of it using them?

Tension on all sides of conflict is rising, pressuring groups who once formed a community to separate, fear one another and engage in a campaign of demonization and violence.

In the age of YouTube, Facebook, and Twitter, conflicts escalate and tension rises at the speed of light, reaching astronomical proportions in matter of minutes and extending the boundaries of conflict rapidly beyond its epicenter.

The most recent explosion of violence between community and law enforcement offers a powerful warning of what lies ahead when polarizing tension is not addressed on either side.

By not harnessing the power of tension between community and police enforcement, critical insights into their disconnect is lost.

In such volatile times as these, traditional negotiating and mediation techniques that aim to compromise are ineffective. Relationships built on commonalities are limiting. They avoid tension. Avoiding tension is a form of censorship because it leaves the conflicting parties feeling unheard, defensive, disenfranchised and hopeless. Each side sees the "other" as irrational and their behavior self-defeating.

Tension is no longer a consequence of the information that is generated. It is information itself.

Recognizing that tension will never be eradicated, a new form of leadership is needed that intentionally uses tension as information to address the mounting pressure surging in all sectors of society: on campuses, in government, in religious institutions, in communities, in businesses and across borders.

This book introduces a paradoxical and evolutionary leadership approach to conflict transformation and cross-cultural communication—Tectonic Leadership. Tectonic comes from the Greek word "to build or create significant change." Brenda and Samia saw a need to create a tectonic shift in how leaders lead and problem-solve. They used earth plate tectonics (the large sections of the earth's surface that shifts) as a metaphor for visualizing human interactions. They recognized that human interactions in situations of conflict are like fault lines between tectonic plates. Plates interact and build friction at their boundaries, causing earthquakes to occur when the natural elasticity of surrounding rocks has been exceeded. Human interactions can similarly create fault lines. When the pressure generated by tension and fear becomes unbearable, the energy released is tsunami-like, creating mass hysteria, inciting hate and fear, separating nations, destroying businesses and communities, oppressing people and instigating wars.

Their leadership model, Tectonic Leadership, harnesses the power of tension and uses tension as an opportunity to inform those in conflict of the deepest fears, pains and trans-generational wounds that separate people in conflict and plague the world.

Human interactions in situations of conflict are like fault lines between tectonic plates.

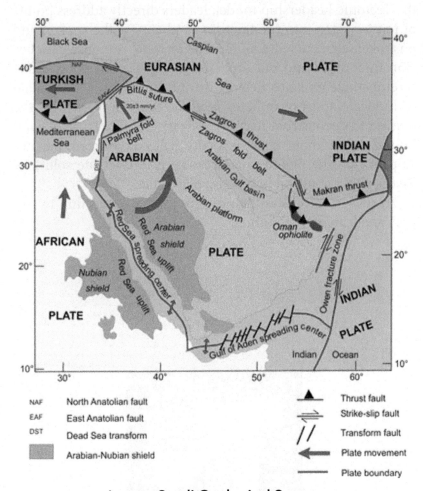

Image: Saudi Geological Survey
(http://www.opinionbug.com/3970/
red-sea-earthquakes%E2%80%94whats-happening/)

Tectonic Leadership brings tension to the table, whether in the dining room, the boardroom or the situation room. Under the Tectonic Leadership model, leaders directly address points of tension, step into the fault line and expose the spoken and unspoken elements of conflict. The tectonic response uses tension to connect and not separate, to engage and not alienate, to empathize and not destroy, to inform and not intimidate, to innovate and not imitate. Tectonic Leaders work with the tension to deconstruct negative narratives, build trust, expand boundaries without changing core belief and create partnerships across the divide to address needs and create solutions that benefit people on both sides of conflict.

Their logo illustrates the power of paired leadership to support and lean on each other.

Why Tectonic Leadership Was Created

The only reason we don't open our hearts and minds to other people is that they trigger confusion in us that we don't feel brave enough or sane enough to deal with it.

Pema Chödrön

Pair of Opposites—Meet Brenda and Samia

Brenda and Samia are not historians, politicians, psychologists or philosophers.

Brenda and Samia are two women from radically different professions, backgrounds, cultures, ideologies and beliefs who share the frustration of unresolved conflict between their opposing communities; two activists alarmed by the lack of effective leadership in these times of high turbulence.

Brenda Rosenberg, left, was the first woman VP of fashion for Hudson's department stores in Michigan, former VP of fashion, merchandizing and marketing for Federated Allied Department stores and developed the fashion merchandizing program for Northwood University in Midland, Michigan. Today, a full-time peacemaker locally and globally. Brenda identifies as a Jewish Zionist and is an active member of AIPAC, the American Israel Political Action Committee. She serves as vice president of the American Jewish Committee in Detroit, Michigan. Brenda is the recipient of 16 local, national and international awards for her interfaith effort. She became the first Jewish woman to give a Ramadan sermon at an American mosque and serves as an ISNA (Islamic Society of North America) panelist on healing the Shia-Sunni divide. Brenda co-authored the book *Friendship & Faith: The WISDOM of women creating alliances for peace* and co-created "Reuniting the Children of Abraham," a multimedia toolkit for peace.

Samia Bahsoun, right, is a telecom executive, international business entrepreneur, secular Muslim, pro-Palestine activist and community organizer. Samia spent most of her adult life building telecommunications networks throughout the world, first as a Research Engineer at Bells laboratories, then as a Telecom Executive and Serial Entrepreneur. She co-founded Capwave Technologies to provide affordable broadband solutions to underserved communities worldwide. Being of Lebanese Muslim descent, born and raised in Dakar (Senegal), an American immigrant since 1979, conversant in Arabic, English, Farsi, French, Spanish, and Wolof, Samia was exposed and sensitized at an early age to issues of race, ethnicity, faith, gender, and politics, becoming an ardent Palestinian rights advocate and anti-Israel militant at the age of 14. As an MIT Sloan EMBA candidate, Samia coaches young Arab entrepreneurs and is a judge for the MIT Enterprise Forum. An immigrant and naturalized American citizen, an entrepreneur in the high-tech sector, a small business owner, Samia is a steering committee member of the NJ Main Street Alliance, promoting policies for innovation, job creation, education, and immigration reform. She is the recipient of the 2013 David Sarnoff Award for Advocacy.

Before Tectonic Leadership

Brenda's Story

I grew up around bright lights. My parents owned the Raven Gallery in Detroit—a meeting place for artists, musicians, writers and civic activists. In my

20s, I began a long career in fashion marketing. I was the first female vice president of fashion merchandizing and marketing for Hudson's in Detroit and went on to become vice president of Federated, Allied department stores. At the chain's height, I identified the trends that would show up in more than 1,000 stores—including Hudson's in Michigan, Bloomingdales in New York, Burdines in Florida and Bullock's in California. I've traveled widely, rubbing shoulders with the rich and famous. I dined in Monaco with Prince Rainier; in Milan with Versace; partied at Regine's in Paris with Bernard Lanvin. I led a dream life for a Jewish girl who loves to shop and party.

But it was the horrific events of 9/11 that changed my life forever. As the towers fell and the death toll mounted, I thought: 'What if I could take my creativity, energy, marketing and merchandising skills and use them to help heal the pains of old and new prejudices, and misconceptions between cultures and religions?'

My thoughts jumped to gold shoes.

Before the late 70s, gold was worn only at night. No women would have even thought of wearing a gold shoe or gold bag during the day. But on a fashion-scouting trip to Saint-Tropez, France I saw a young woman lunching at Le Club 55, sporting gold loafers with her jeans. I saw money. Big money. I wanted a pair, and I knew in an instant that every women and every little girl would too. **"Gold by Day"** *became J. L. Hudson's big fall campaign.*

"Gold by Day" was one of my most daring marketing successes.

We made shoe history. It was a huge success. To this day, women and young girls wear "Gold by Day."

"Gold By Day"

It was the success of this paradoxical concept of "Gold by Day" that gave me the courage to go beyond the common sense of what others said was impossible.

That day, I started building partnerships. In Metro Detroit, the most segregated city in America, we created unprecedented relationships between Christians, Jews and Muslims. Together, we created "Reuniting the Children of Abraham," a multimedia toolkit for peace. In over 124 presentations we brought together individuals and communities that never would have met without the program.

Nothing in the business world prepared me for the courage I needed to have in doing this work. I feel I walk on dental floss between communities. As a Jewish woman who cares deeply for our Jewish community and is passionate about Israel's survival, I had no idea that what I saw as bridge-building

*would be seen as controversial, nor did I ever antic-
ipate the severe criticism I received.*

*I thought I would get hugs from our community,
but I have also received threats and have been spit
on. Some Jews call me naive to call for ceasefire,
and some of my Arab friends thought I was way
too soft on Israel, especially during the 2009 war
between Israel and Gaza. The death and destruction created a polarizing rift no ordinary dialogue
could bridge.*

*I called my friend and teacher Debbie Ford. I asked
if she knew an Arab coach I could partner with.
Debbie said to call Samia Bahsoun. I sent Samia
an email introduction and we set a time to talk.*

Samia's Story

*Before I tell you how Brenda and I connected, I
need to tell you where I was before I met Brenda,
five years ago.*

*Five years ago, I was totally disillusioned about
any possibility of conflict resolution in the region,
let alone finding a partner on the other side. I
was angry ... very angry with Israel for killing my
grandmother and aunt, who were burned to death
during Israeli air raids on southern Lebanon in
1982. I was angry with my Jewish neighbors and
friends for standing with Israel when they raided
Lebanon again in 2006.*

*If I were invited to speak to you five years ago, I
would have given you "our" reasons for kidnapping
three Israeli soldiers and argued that Israel used it as
an excuse to bomb Lebanon and intended to attack
all along. I would have defended my community
and myself and argued for the many imprisoned
Lebanese who have been fighting Israeli occupation*

of southern Lebanon.

I am, in fact, pretty good at arguing! I started arguing and advocating against Israel and for the Palestinians at the age of 14. During my last year in high school, I remember destroying grapefruits produced in Israel at the school cafeteria counter so no one could consume them. In college, I rallied and organized against Israel. I often found myself in the front row of a demonstration against Israel and Zionism.

There was a small period of time where I found the will to meet the other side and actually had hope. When I joined AT&T Bell Laboratories in New Jersey in 1985, I began to work with research scientists from Israel and agreed to participate in a dialogue group organized by the Foundation for Middle East Communication at the invitation of a Canadian colleague. Meeting the other helped temper my anger, but the mounting tension in the region, especially the war in 2006, took me right back to where I was in my teens. I had little hope that our people could ever come to an agreement, let alone coexist with them.

This was until 2009 when I received a phone call from a certain Brenda Rosenberg. A phone call that will forever change the way I look at conflict. A phone call that altered my relationship with the other, my relationship with tension.

 **TECTONIC LEADERSHIP EXERCISE**

Identify someone you feel is an "other" or even an enemy.
What separates you?
What would you need to feel safe meeting with that person?
What are the obstacles to make this meeting happen?

_____

_____

_____

_____

_____

_____

_____

_____

_____

_____

"Two opposing truths can exist simultaneously
in the same space. Do not therefore assume
that that which opposes you is that which is not
good for you. It may be just the reverse."
Niels Bohr

A Tectonic Conversation

The reason for evil in the world today is that people are not able to tell their stories.

Carl Jung

What Ford did not predict is that, despite their years of training and a shared interest in ending conflict, Brenda and Samia were faced with an ideological barrier, insurmountable to many.

At the epicenter of conflict

Brenda called Samia: "Hi, I am Brenda; I am a Jewish Zionist who is devastated by the ongoing war between Israel and Gaza. I am very concerned about both the Palestinians and the Israelis."

All Samia heard was that Brenda identified as a "Zionist." She immediately dismissed Brenda's concern about both countries' citizens.

How can a Zionist care about anyone else other than a Jew? she asked herself. For Samia, the Zionists were the invaders—they were the terrorists. Samia, who lost her grandmother and aunt to Israeli raids in southern Lebanon in 1982, and whose family was displaced during the July 2006 Israeli on Lebanon, saw these wars as Zionist expansion disguised under an Israeli self-defense campaign following the Holocaust.

Samia, like most Arabs, saw Zionism as the ultimate tension point in the Arab-Israeli conflict. From the get-go, Samia was not the bit least interested about engaging Brenda further. She chose this opportunity to ask Brenda one of her burning questions:

"Why can't the Jews give up the Holocaust story and move on?"

Suddenly, there was total silence. This was where most conversations between Jews and Arabs end. Brenda took a deep breath.

"Why would you ask me to give up the Holocaust?"

Samia replied without hesitation: "Because of the pain it has caused and continues to cause Palestinians and Arabs in the [Middle East] region for a crime they did not commit."

Auschwitz
Photo: *KZ Dachau*

Brenda replied: "Samia, after 10 years of Jewish-Arab dialogue, no one has ever said that to me. I never saw the depth of the human tragedy of the Holocaust from the Arab perspective; I have only seen it through the death of the six million Jews and millions of others annihilated by the Nazis."

Brenda began to understand. Not only were six million Jews brutally killed, millions of Palestinians and Jews were forced to become refugees. Jews and Palestinians were both chased from their homes and exiled from Arab countries. Both were displaced and afraid.

Brenda said: "We must never forget any aspect of the horror."

Lebanon under Israeli Raids
Photo: EPA/WAEL HAMZEH

A Tectonic Moment

We are at a critical moment in history. We can choose to self-destruct or create new discourse and be in the presence of the best of our humanity.

Brenda & Samia

As Brenda acknowledged tension from both sides, instead of avoiding the tension and advocating for her side only, she created the space for Samia to open up. Samia responded:

"So how can we use the Holocaust to heal humanity and prevent future genocides instead of having the Holocaust use us?"

The conversation shifted, and they began to collaborate:

"How can we use the past, instead of the past using us? How can we use our pain to end conflict instead of the pain using us to perpetuate conflict? How can we use tension to bridge our differences and connect our humanity instead of allowing tension to separate us and destroy us?"

This insight became the mantra of their future interactions.

How tension transformed conflict

Brenda and Samia began their journey as tension warriors with this mantra as their anchor.

As they tackled the hot topics that separated their communities—Zionism, the Holocaust, Gaza, the Lebanon War, Jerusalem, occupation, settlements, suicide bombing, the right of return, the international flotilla to Gaza, etc., they applied their mantra and used the tension of polarized perceptions of these events to deepen their understanding of each other. They saw the importance of connecting the death of 70-year-old Holocaust victim Dora Shaklyan, who died at Teofipol in Ukraine, to the death of Samia's 70-year-old grandmother, Mariam Bahsoun, who was a victim of Israeli raids in Tyre, without comparing the pain and suffering against one another. They expanded the Holocaust story to include both narratives.

They recognized the barriers that separate Israelis and Palestinians are not just physical, but emotionally charged, complex and fueled by current events. These events could have been used to demonize each other. Or, they could shift the attention to finding new solutions together.

Brenda and Samia had a choice: they could remain stuck in the status quo of most dialogue groups and diplomatic efforts and use each current news event to reinforce and advance their own narrative. They could talk about the trauma and destruction of the Israelis and Palestinians, blaming the other side.

Or, they could take a different course of action.

They became relentless in the search for a course of action that would make a difference.

Years of emotional education and "shadow" work with Debbie Ford added the skill of comprehending their "shadows"—"the unconscious part of themselves that was deemed bad or wrong." They understood their capacity to deceive, harm and even terrorize. Their work with Debbie also enhanced understanding mutually held fears of being misunderstood, hurt and annihilated by the other.

As they coached each other, it soon became apparent that they were holding on to a gripping subconscious—or, as Debbie Ford called it, an "underlying" commitment that was greater than the commitment to peace. This subconscious commitment to the pain shaped a shared identity and a common mantra:

Are we using the suffering endured by both our people to inspire justice, reconnect with the other and end the conflict, or is the pain using us to create more harm, separate us further and perpetuate the conflict?

Embracing tension soon deepened their understanding of the other and deconstructed negative narratives. From here, Brenda and Samia created a joint narrative, bridging the divide and innovating new solutions that benefitted both communities.

Over the past five years, thousands of hours of challenging telephone conversations and email exchanges have been shared on the most contested "hot topics" of the Middle East. Despite their training and willingness to listen, these conversations sometimes became contentious; at times the anger was too loud, the pain too great. Buttons got pushed—barriers often seemed insurmountable. Long silences created anxiety. At times, the phone stopped ringing. Fault lines formed again.

Brenda and Samia had a choice:

Stay silent, grow further apart, deepen the gap and witness Israelites and Palestinians collide—or, be the example of how fault lines can be transformed, boundaries re-examined and expanded, and relationships created and sustained.

The phone lines remain open to this day. With each call, faults are exposed, attentions are redirected, feelings are acknowledged and boundaries are expanded. Barriers intertwined yield to visions intertwined. While their relationship was originally defined by judgment and blame, it became a relationship of trust and personal responsibility.

Since that first phone call, contentious events have not been spared. Would a nuclear Iran be a threat or provide balance? Is Hezbollah a terrorist organization or liberator? Can Israel be a Jewish state and be democratic?

Paired and committed, Brenda and Samia step together into the fault line, probe below the surface, examine the tension and use it to deepen understanding and explore new solutions.

TL TECTONIC LEADERSHIP EXERCISE

Recall a time when you were faced with a
challenging conversation with someone and
either ended the conversation OR reacted and
defended your position?

_____

_____

_____

_____

_____

_____

_____

_____

_____

 **TECTONIC LEADERSHIP EXERCISE**

What would that same conversation be like if you allowed the space for the other person to fully express themselves?

_____

_____

_____

_____

_____

_____

_____

_____

_____

_____

_____

Harnessing the Power of Tension In Business

How changing Your Relationship With Tension Can Increase Your Market Share

Story by Samia M. Bahsoun

A few years ago, a Fortune 500 telecommunications supplier recruited me to market one of their products in China. This Fortune 500 company—let's call it Company A—pioneered the technology and needed me to market it as a member of the developing team.

Three other companies were tailgating Company A. Company B had come up with a new product that provided more bandwidth than Company A's product. They were able to pack twice as many channels into the same spectrum without impairing quality. And while Company A had the knowledge to do same, they had come to market three years earlier and needed to recover their investment before committing the factory to building a new product.

Furthermore, China was concurrently deploying a new nationwide fiber optic network. It was the largest market to be had by any company, and the competition was fierce! After the first round of elimination, four companies were shortlisted. They knew price was not going to be the only differentiator—companies were ready to give up their product at cost and below cost to gain first access to the huge Chinese market.

Company A's product had been deployed in other markets, but delivered half the capacity of Company B. Soon, Company

B leapfrogged the first generation of products and came into market for the first time with a higher performing product.

Tension 1: Company A delivers half the bandwidth offered by the competition!

As Company A's technical marketing agent, I found myself delivering an inferior solution (half the bandwidth). After the first round of grueling question and answer sessions with the most select engineers, we found that we made it through. The session was in Chinese, so I had an interpreter at all times. By the end of the first round, I could pace myself with the interpreter like keys on a music sheet.

The second round was held in a smaller room. A handful of senior management and senior technical advisors sat on the buyer side of the table. Once again, I was told that the Q-and-A would be in Chinese and I was provided with an interpreter.

I started by introducing the company and our product. I knew that technically we were at a loss with Company B.

Tectonic Leadership principle: "Understand that tension is never eradicated."

I decided, without consulting my client, Company A, to tackle the problem head on by acknowledging that our product delivered half the bandwidth. I paused and waited for the interpreter, who worked for Company A, to translate. He uttered a few words and glared at me, eyes wide open. I knew then that he did not interpret what I had just said. I repeated the message and asked him to translate again. I noticed at that point that the decision maker on the buyer side smiled, indicating that he indeed understood English. I knew then that I had built trust with the buyer.

Tectonic Leadership principle: " Use the tension to connect and not separate"

Tension was out in the open. By exposing the fault, I established trust. I knew that my next step was to use the tension to inform and connect with the buyer. In order to do this, I needed to commit to "care equally for self and other" and reinforce trust.

At this moment, I was no longer focused on promoting and defending Company A's product, but meeting the buyer's needs.

I knew the Chinese were developing their infrastructure and introducing this technology for the first time into their market. I learned through the first round of questioning that they only needed a third of the bandwidth we were offering for the next three years. Our product at this point met their current and future bandwidth needs. By the time they were going to reach capacity exhaust, Company A would have leapfrogged Company B's product at least eight times the capacity, which was already in Company A's product roadmap for the future.

I also learned from our initial U.S. product deployment that network features were just as important as network reliability. Why would it be any different for the Chinese? I decided to share our experience and concerns with Company A when we deployed the product in the U.S. market. Then, I shifted the conversation again from what they "thought" they wanted (the latest, greatest and lowest cost) to what they needed (enough capacity and a reliable network). While the buyer needed to deploy a certain amount of bandwidth in its new network, they needed to make sure that the product they were going to buy would work and that the network would be robust and reliable for a strong customer experience. While there are contractual penalties if the supplier does not meet the requirements, a network failure could mean that the buyer can lose its customer—and no contractual penalties can remedy customer churn. Bandwidth was important, but robustness was equally important.

Tension 2: Boosting network robustness!

Up to this point, I did not bash either Company B, or C or D or F. I addressed the tension and focused on the needs of the buyer. Robustness is where Company A had an advantage. Their product had been deployed and operational for over three years in the U.S. market by large network operators. All other companies were tailgating Company A, and Company B's product had just come to market.

At this point, I addressed the key points of tension in the buyer's mind. I started by:

1. Exposing the fault
2. Addressing the tension
3. Caring more for the buyer than Company A
4. Using the tension to understand and meet the needs of the buyer, build trust and connect with the buyer
5. Focusing on finding solutions together by addressing the current needs
6. Presenting a roadmap for future needs.

The buyer invited us to dinner. One of their senior managers approached me and thanked me for my honesty. Company A gained 87 percent of the Chinese market that year!

By using tension (to inform myself of the buyer's needs and inform the buyer of our product) instead of having the tension use me (by advocating for our product and against the competitor through hiding facts), we were able to secure not only a large market with Company A's current product but also a market for their subsequent product releases.

TECTONIC LEADERSHIP EXERCISE

How can you use the six points outlined on the previous page in your business?

_____

_____

_____

_____

_____

_____

_____

_____

_____

_____

We don't have to see eye to eye to work together.

Harnessing the Power of Tension at the Negotiating Table

Tension is the primary creative force behind the manifestation of any outcome. It is as natural, as powerful as the force of gravity.

David Emerald

The September 2012 U.N. Conference on Palestinian Statehood and Durban III is just one example of a missed opportunity to apply a Tectonic approach to conflict transformation. Leaders from across the board fell into the "fight or flight" trap. Palestinians presented it as a "fight" for their denied identity, but the Israeli saw it as "fighting" against it as a threat to their security. Both parties "fled" from the peace process. Their respective allies did not respond any differently. The veto by the United States was a "flight" response to the fear of alienating its ally in the region, broadening the divide.

Reactions to the Durban III U.N. Conference that followed were no different. Australia, Canada, the United States, Israel, the Czech Republic, Italy and the Netherlands announced that they would boycott Durban III, charging that the Durban process has been used to promote racism, intolerance, anti-Semitism and Holocaust denial, and to erode freedom of speech and Israel's right to exist. Such a boycott unfortunately does not address the tension surrounding these issues, widening the divide. Both are "fighting" for what they believe to be right. Both are "flee-ing" to the comfort of those who share the same point of view instead of addressing the fear and issues that create the tension between people whose views are different.

What could have changed if the Israeli and the Palestinians worked through the Tectonic Leadership process and did not walk away?

The following pages demonstrate how Samia and Brenda mapped the U.N. Conference on Palestinian statehood using the Tectonic Leadership process.

Tectonic Leadership Process:

Harnessing the Power of Tension
to Build Alliances

1. Name the tension that is dividing you

Be direct and honest with each other and communicate the tensions that divide you.

Palestinians going to U.N. for statehood recognition, in addition to direct negotiations with the State of Israel.

2. Describe the tension on each side

All parties in conflict are given permission to clearly express their feelings surrounding the situation of tension without feeling criticized or censored.

Exercise:

1. Describe the situation of tension
2. Name your feelings: angry, hurt, disappointed, frustrated, helpless, hopeless, uncomfortable, impatient, overwhelmed, etc.

Each side names the people representing them at the negotiating table. All parties affected by the conflict must be represented.

Palestinian tension: Not recognized as a full member state. Feel frustrated, angry, disenfranchised. Not working on an even playing field. How can we negotiate if we are not recognized as a state?

Israeli tension: Went to the U.N. instead of direct negotiations. Feel that there is no partner on the other side. Who are we negotiating with? The Palestinian Authority of Abbas or Hamas?

3. Bridge the Divide by Harnessing the Power of Tension

The intent is to develop a new relationship with tension by:
- Understanding that tension will never be eradicated.
- Expanding boundaries without changing core beliefs, knowing that one can validate the feelings of the other without agreeing with the other.
- Harnessing the power of tension to connect and not separate, utilizing tension as an opportunity to deconstruct negative narratives and deepen understanding rather than as an obstacle in partnering.

Exercise:

1. What could you say to the other to express your position and your pain?

Palestinian Need: Need to be recognized as an independent and contiguous Palestinian state.

Israeli Need: Need to be recognized as a Jewish state, living in safety and security.

2. How can you respond to the other, recognizing their position and pain?

Palestinians: Work with Israelis to understand what it means for Israel to be a Jewish state and articulate what safety and security means for Israelis.

Israelis: Work with Palestinians to understand what an equal state means for them and what would be the status of Palestinians living in Israel.

3. What could you say to the other that would engage them, inspire them to work with you and bring a new level of mutual understanding?

- Together, declare which policies and which projects you would be willing to support and implement to benefit both communities.
- Together, create a plan on how each solution will be executed, setting specific goals and milestones.
- Hold each other accountable to both communities.

4. What could you say to the other that would build trust and hope that together, as partners, it is possible to create a safe and just future for your communities and all of humanity?

4. Lead Tectonically by Harnessing the Power of Tension

- Partner with someone from the opposite side of conflict—tectonic partners hold each other accountable to stay committed to the relationship, especially during times of crisis.
- Tectonic partners willingly stand with each other and engage both communities. They actualize a shared congruent identity without changing core beliefs.

Concrete Action Steps:

1. Find a partner on the other side and commit together to the disciplines and commitments of Tectonic Leadership.
2. Together, create a project that would benefit both parties, knowing that each party might have different needs.
3. Create a plan that includes:
   a. Your vision, goals and milestones
   b. A list of obstacles you foresee and the resources you might need to mitigate them
   c. A support structure to assure sustainability

Create policies and laws that:

- *Reject and condemn the teaching of hate, contempt, disrespect, incitement and violence; all acts of violence, oppression, degradation, humiliation, and injustice; all acts of terrorism, bombing, and murders of innocent civilians irrespective of nationality or religion*
- *Support the right of every person to live in freedom, with dignity, equality and justice; two independent states living peacefully side by side, thus ending the conflict and occupation.; that all Holy Places are protected, secure, and accessible to everyone*
- *Implement some of the following programs:*
- *Create joint Israeli-Palestinian task force of scholars that would write together the history of Middle East for classrooms with particular focus on Israel and Palestine*
- *Negotiate long-term water sharing agreements*
  Encourage free trade with both a new Palestinian state and Israel
     - *Promote Israeli and Palestinian access to world markets*

TECTONIC LEADERSHIP EXERCISE

Are you willing to understand others first, and be heard second?

Are you willing to validate others truth when it is different from yours?

What are you willing to create or work for that will benefit both sides of the conflict?

_____

_____

_____

_____

_____

_____

_____

_____

_____

Tension Will Never Be Eradicated

Tension is no longer a consequence of the information that is generated; it is information itself.

Samia and Brenda

Segregation knows no frontier. It exists in both large and small cities in the U.S. and around the globe. Every city has an east and a west, a north and a south. These are not just cardinal points on a map. hey are demarcation lines of communities divided by economics, race, culture and religion and span generations to become part of the DNA of today's society—a "new normal."

By pairing people across these lines and articulating and comprehending the root causes of tension, tectonic leaders can break the destructive pattern of stereotyping that leads to demonizing and dehumanizing the other and leverage the soft and hard assets of each community and neighborhood.

Tension in the Age of Facebook, YouTube and Twitter

Leading the way to cool conversations on hot topics

Story by Vivian Henoch, Editor MyJewishDetroit

Tectonic Leadership inspired two of its alumni, Teri Bazzi-Olivier and Ariana Mentzel, to develop a social media spin that puts forth "Tectonic Tips" for Cool Conversations on Hot Topics.

Teri and Ariana met and collaborated at the first Tectonic retreat in 2011. A passionate speaker and thoughtful writer, Teri, is a busy "soccer" mom of three, a recent graduate in English and African American Studies from the University of Michigan Dearborn and self-described in her blog as an American-Muslim, Irish-Arab who loves religion and all things (well most things) Middle Eastern. Ariana, is an Israeli American, a graduate of Michigan State University with a B.A. in International Studies, and an M.A. in Diplomacy and Conflict Studies from the Lauder School of Government at the Interdisciplinary Center in Herzliya, Israel. Dedicated to interfaith work since her graduation, Ariana has traveled to Abu Dhabi as part of the American Jewish Committee's young women's delegation at the Women as Global Leaders Conference at Zayed University in 2012. In 2013, she attended the Muslim Jewish Conference in Sarajevo, Bosnia and Herzegovina. Recently married, living in Beverly Hills, Michigan, Ariana currently is an instructor in First Year Hebrew at Michigan State University.

"It all started because we were bickering on Facebook," recalls Teri.

"We'd been friends for three years—considered ourselves Tectonic leaders," observed Ariana, "but, on Facebook, we suddenly found a whole other side of one another that we didn't like. In social media, there's a different truth."

"We weren't being very Tectonic," said Teri with a chuckle. "Our conversation quickly degenerated on the topic of Israel and Palestine."

As both women sat behind their computers fuming, fanning the flames of their Facebook messages back and forth, they suddenly realized they had to put a stop to the public debate and sit down together for a discussion face-to-face.

Teri: "We were speaking the same language, but we discovered we couldn't agree even on the meaning of words we were using."

Ariana: "We were talking about 'human shields' and found that the term, itself, meant two very different things to us. I'm saying Hamas is using Gazans as human shields while Teri is saying, yes, but it's the Israelis who are using Gazans as human shields … so you start to see how words can be loaded terms. People can have the same conversation and walk away not understanding anything, unless you explain exactly what your words mean."

Teri: "Of course, that kind of discretion and definition doesn't happen in online. We could argue about the terms of human shields, terrorism and occupation forever and never see eye-to-eye. But what we can do is to stop the cycle of argument and start to create responsible social media."

Ariana: "So we made a pact with one another."

Teri: "Then we made a pledge … "

Ariana: "Which brought us to our project: a social media platform we call Tectonic Tips for Cool Conversations on Hot Topics."

Teri: "We've come up with this term, 'spoilers,' meaning those who have an agenda to stir up anger, fear and hate. Our objective in creating Tectonic Tips for Cool Conversations on Hot Topics is to decrease the number of 'spoilers' out there. Overall, our goal is to create a movement of social media users committed and disciplined to change their discourse on hot topics—such as the Holocaust and the Israel-Palestine conflict—and to move from debate and blame to active engagement on both sides in finding new solutions, common purpose and harmony."

Ariana: "I made a vow—to be responsible for what I read online. When I want to know what Israelis are saying about the conflict, I look at their official websites; when I want to know what Hamas is saying, I look at their website. And when I want commentary, I read Gershon Baskin, who was a negotiator in freeing Gilad Shalit."

The game plan for social media responsibility

With the support of the American Jewish Committee (AJC) and the Michigan Muslim Community Council, Brenda, Teri and Ariana have an action plan to take Tectonic Tips on the road, in presentations to area churches, mosques, synagogues and community groups.

Talking across divides

Harnessing the Power of Tension at Home

Story by David Crumm

David Crumm is a journalist and author who is a specialist in cross-cultural reporting in the U.S., Europe, the Middle East and Asia.

"It's time to change my life. We're going to eat differently, starting today."

Has your loved one ever made an announcement like this? I've made such a declaration to my wife—in fact, too many times to count. I've also been on the receiving end of these declarations. My wife is a Lifetime Member of Weight Watchers and has followed other weight-loss programs, as well. I jumped into Weight Watchers several times, although I never got as far as in the program as my more-committed wife. So, we're both veterans of this kind of strong-willed commitment to shaping up through changing what we eat. And between such high-spirited campaigns? We slide back into comfortable eating habits.

Perhaps in your home, a declaration about changing one's life through diet is driven by a different goal. Perhaps it isn't simply a desire to lose weight. Your partner may have decided to give up red meat—or to adopt a strictly vegetarian diet. Perhaps your partner is diabetic and declares: No more sugar! Maybe a no-salt diet is the goal. Maybe, horror of horrors for type-A men and women: No more caffeine in your home! Perhaps your partner has decided you should follow Kosher food laws—or adopt a number of other traditional dietary codes.

Most likely, this is a moment of great emotion—and great pride. Partners want to lovingly support each other in such a noble pursuit. But this also can be a moment of stark terror if you're on the receiving end. Think about the declaration again: "It's time to change *my* life. *We're* going to eat differently, starting today." Perhaps the words you've spoken—or you've heard—vary slightly. But let's be honest: usually, the declaration comes from one partner—who proudly wants the other to come on board this life-changing journey.

"We have to do this together." That's what we say, or we hear from our partner. And that makes a lot of sense. Most couples share the 'fridge, the evening meal, the leftovers.

But, most homes also run on rituals that tap into our most primeval hunter-gatherer need for the reassurance of food. With a sudden declaration from a loved one that comfort foods are being snatched from our fingertips—perhaps forever—anxiety fuels conflict. It's such a turbulent swirl of emotions! We want to support our partner's declaration, made in pursuit of health and vitality—or perhaps a deepening of faith. If you suddenly find yourself as an anchor dragging this ship backwards—then stubbornness soon mingles with shame and even bitterness at this partner who suddenly is ready for a daring cruise into new waters. Like steel scraping stone, even the best of intentions can scatter a shower of sparks through your household each day. Usually it happens when the partner who is "going along" on this journey reaches that moment in the day when a doughnut, a salty pretzel, a hot mug of coffee or a cheesy peperoni pizza becomes, at first, a pang and quickly builds into an all-consuming desire.

Over the years, in the first week after my wife declares a new dietary regimen, I may quite literally reach for a bag of greasy-salty-wonderful potato chips, or that last scoop of ice cream in the freezer, or a final midnight snack of that last soft-and-chewy chocolate-chip cookie.

At the sound of crinkling wrappers or an opening freezer door, her voice echoes through the house: "Are you eating!?!"

Even if I say, "No, but I was tempted," and yank my wandering hand from its offending goal, blood pressures already are rising.

She wonders: *Could he be eating on the sly? Why isn't he committed to this? He's undermining me! And, now, because he was tempted—I'm tempted to cheating, too!*

I'm thinking: *Why is she yelling at me! I love her and, sure, the goal is good—but my life is stressful enough without trying to do this, right now! Is she already suspicious that I'm sneaking cookies? Well, if she's suspicious, then maybe I should grab just one. But, no ...*

On and on. The impulses and the hot exchanges are reprised each day. What began as a noble goal and a grand declaration brings anxiety, suspicion and inevitably: tension.

One option is simply to let those sparks fly, which certainly wouldn't help either of us overcome our daily stress let alone inch toward our dietary goals. After nearly 40 years of marriage, we've learned how to turn this corner and the key is to honestly acknowledge the tension. It's there. There's no point in denying it—and talking openly helps us to clear the air.

So, now, we begin such journeys by telling each other our daily stories of temptation and frustration. Then, we work together to reorganize our home. One of my temptations? Cookies. They call to me with a sweet serenade late in the evening. But, for her? Cookies are nothing! Her chief temptation? Buttery popcorn. A hot, freshly popped bag is the perfect way to unwind—the messier the fingertips, the better. But, for me? I don't like popcorn. Not a clue why that's appealing.

Just talking about the lure of these treats—rather than feuding over them—can actually turn to laughter. "You're panicking over a cookie? Really?" Or I might say: "Popcorn is haunting you? Really?" And, of course, we can reassure ourselves that we're not giving up these treats forever. In fact, in moderation, they can remain a part of a healthy diet. We're soon in this together—facing our demons together, once again.

It's in honestly admitting that tension exists that we begin any dietary journey now. And, together, we clear out the candy bowl, empty the cookie jar, dump the ice cream from the freezer, clean out the last box of extra-butter popcorn from the pantry. Is it easy? Of course not. But we now know how to embark on this dietary journey, confront the inevitable conflict head on—and sail through it together.

Harnessing the Power of Tension Between Roommates

Story by Cody Terrance Harrell

Cody Terrance Harrell is a journalism and English teacher in Michigan, and a recent graduate of Michigan State University. Cody was the editor and designer of this book.

I like to think I'm a reasonable roommate.

I tend to keep to myself, unless I'm incessantly screaming at a Michigan State football game or reading English 11 position papers and need someone to keep my head above the waters of standards-based grading.

I try to keep my room consistently clean, if you don't count the sticky mess of gels and pastes that connects my bathroom sink and the counter space that I grudgingly clean every three months or so when it starts to tug on my toothbrush handle. Again, if you don't count that, I'm golden.

I usually won't leave my things in the living room, I clean up after myself when I do the dishes, I even fold my laundry the day the same day that I throw it through the washer and dryer.

Again, fairly reasonable.

And when I agreed to move in with my best friend and his wonderful fiancée in the fall following graduation, I expected the best. While he and I hadn't lived together since our freshman year in college, I figured that his picture-perfect engagement encouraged him to at least try and grow up—even slightly— from our Landon Hall dog days.

I even convinced myself that his days of staying up half the night playing loud video games—even with headphones on— and leaving his blindingly bright LED lamp shining perfectly through the slats of my lofted bed and into my eyes were in the past.

And as I walked confidently into our new apartment, noticing the bright gleam of the walls and embracing the clean smell that adorned every nook and cranny of the apartment, I again reassured myself that this would be the perfect living situation. Knowing good and well that I would get my own bedroom, bathroom and closet, I sincerely believed that any of our minimal problems would be easily overcome as a happy triplet of roommates.

Well, you called it. I was wrong.

The first month was fine—or so I thought. While I spent most of my time drinking espresso and working on a plethora of summer projects with my soon-departing friends in our last summer together, I began to notice changing habits.

Not exactly for the better.

After returning home from an evening with friends, I'd come home to a sink piled to the brim with filthy pans, pots, mugs, plates, silverware and bowls covered in every type of food product imaginable. And not only was the sink full, but the trashcan stood overflowing—with no one seeming to take mind of the severity of the smell. This piqued the interest of the cat, who found a chip bag to be a more adventurous toy than a lobster on a stick.

Even our original agreements started to fall apart as we settled in through the first couple of months.

While they agreed to cook if I paid a third of the grocery bill, I came home most nights to finished pans of food or empty bowls and plates "saved" for me.

While I agreed to do a majority of the dishes, I would find plates and bowls coated and crusted with cheese, oatmeal and other unforgivables stowed away or left in the living room, hours away from being able to be reasonably cleaned without steel wool and an iron will.

I was, figuratively and literally, fed up.

And when I began working with Brenda and saw Tectonic Leadership in action, I noticed that these tensions were affecting both of us in negative ways. We were avoiding the tension with each other and ignored the fault lines that separated us like the space between the countertop and the fridge—where most scraps go to die.

I changed my attitude towards them almost immediately. Instead of trying to compromise, I brought them both together and expressed my frustrations verbally and in person, rather than harboring my annoyance and venting it onto my other friends.

I found that I was not the only one with pent-up frustration.

While I thought myself the reasonable roommate, my best friends saw it very, very differently. What I saw as a lack of providing dinner scraps, they saw as a lack of interest in spending time with them and adhering to a "normal" daily routine. What I saw as spending time with my friends before they left town, they saw as abandoning daily household chores and being an anti-social roommate.

It became clear to me in those moments that these tensions could not be avoided. No matter what compromise I could have prepared, I would have ignored their need to use a plethora of dishes and quickly fill the garbage can to the brim on a weekly basis with necessary "items" that I would normally not purchase. They have always lived that way, and I cannot ask to change that about them.

However, together, we began to use the tension as a point of conversation and change. We drew up brand new responsibilities, with expectations for all parties that each roommate would abide by to make the experience more enjoyable for all.

And while we fail to adhere to these rules in isolated incidents, harnessing the power of tension helped the most unlikely of trios create an open and honest atmosphere with each other through acknowledging our differences, without sacrificing our ideals. Tectonic Leadership turned our anxiety into action.

TECTONIC LEADERSHIP EXERCISE

What "food tensions" or "roommate tensions" have you experienced?

_____

_____

_____

_____

_____

_____

_____

_____

_____

_____

_____

Bridge
To form a connection between two points.
Synonyms: Join, link, connect, unite, reconcile

Tectonic Leadership for Systemic Change

*You cannot build a bridge without points of tension.
Without tension the bridge will collapse.*

Samia and Brenda

Knowing that tension will never be eradicated, Brenda and Samia asked:

What if tension is no longer the enemy?

What would it look like if we lead people directly into the fault line and use the tension that once separated us to deepen our understanding of the other?

What type of commitment and discipline is required to create systemic change?

What type of leadership is needed to change the course of history in time of constant turbulence?

To answer these questions, they created a leadership roadmap for governments, businesses and organizations: Tectonic Leadership for Systemic Change.

The tectonic response to fear connects and does not separate, engages and does not alienate, empathizes and does not destroy. The two sides in conflict are like two tectonic plates converging upon one another. Neither wants to break, nor give. For the rocks to gain their former elasticity at the fault line, each side must move beyond fight or flight and use tension as an opportunity to inform each other of the deepest fears, pains and trans-generational wounds that separate people in conflict and plague the world. Tectonic leaders build trust and create a new discourse.

Tectonic Leadership's paradoxical and revolutionary approach to leadership offers a vehicle for developing pairs of leaders from opposite sides of conflict to facilitate cross-cultural understanding and transform conflict. It provides leaders with the structure, discipline and commitment to create together the foundation for a "new relational architecture" that sustains seismic events inherent to today's civilization.

Tectonic Leadership goes beyond identifying commonalities between people in conflict. Tectonic Leadership directly addresses and utilizes the tension between people from opposite sides of conflict and provides them with the structure, discipline and commitment to find new solutions together.

When Samia asked Brenda why Jews don't give up the Holocaust and move on, she was not aware about how Brenda would feel. In fact, she sent her a message articulating that she did not really care about how Brenda felt. Samia's intentions were not consciously malicious, but her attention to advocating for herself, her community, the Palestinians and the Lebanese that suffered under Israeli aggression—and dismissing Jewish pain without fully understanding it—resulted in destructive impact. It took a real commitment from Brenda to even ask:

"Samia, why would you ask me to give up the Holocaust story?"

Brenda then gave Samia space amidst the tension to express herself and the opportunity to inform Brenda. Brenda could have easily hung up the phone and walked away. She probably wouldn't have heard from Samia again, who would have reverted back to her former mindset—only this time with a greater certainty that there is no partner on the other side.

While they couldn't keep natural disasters from happening, they had a choice: remain silent, grow further apart and deepen the gap—or, live as an example of how fault lines can be transformed with re-examined and expanded boundaries.

They made the decision to stay committed to each other and inspire each other in times of tension.

On February 14, 2009, Aasiya Z. Hassan, 37, was beheaded in Buffalo, New York, by her husband, Mussamil Hassan, 44. Mussamil was the CEO of Bridges TV, a Muslim TV station the couple created together to produce a more positive image of Islam for Americans. Three years before the incident, Aasiya was at Brenda's house filming an interview with Brenda and Imam Abdullah El Amin for a one-hour TV special, "Reuniting the Children of Abraham," their multimedia toolkit for peace.

Brenda's first reaction to the beheading was deeply rooted in fear. She felt that it was no longer safe to work with Muslims, who lived in a culture that she thought justified honor killing. Obviously shaken by the incident, Brenda called Samia to inform her and was prepared to call it quits with the Muslim community. When Brenda realized that Samia's reaction mirrored hers, calling it quits was no longer an option. Instead, they agreed to speak together to both communities about the horror of the incident instead of demonizing Muslims.

From their discussions of real life situations of conflict, they learned key ideals to transform conflict:

> Do not need to give up your core beliefs and identity. Instead, expand your identity and create a shared congruent identity;
>
> Change your relationship with tension and harness its power to connect, not separate. Deepen your knowledge and understanding of each other;
>
> Commit to lead together through the lens of evolution, not through the lens of survival. Become dedicated to walking a path where there are no footprints, a a. path now delineated by their joint purpose to create change that benefits both communities.

These three elements became the driving force of the Tectonic Leadership Model for conflict transformation and cross-cultural communication.

The 3 Disciplines and Commitments of Tectonic Leadership

1. Tectonic leaders collaborate with opposing sides of conflict and take joint ownership in transforming conflict

Tectonic leaders expand their boundaries and create a shared congruent identity without changing their core beliefs. Tectonic leaders do not focus solely on advocating for only one side. Tectonic leaders commit to a level of integrity that cares equally about self and other. They face challenges together and seek solutions together.

2. Tectonic leaders know that tension is never eradicated and do not avoid tension. Rather, they use tension surrounding conflict as an opportunity to deepen their understanding of the other and engage the other

Tectonic Leaders do not react to tension generated by mistrust, lack of respect, unmet expectations, denial of identity, targeted aggression, and current events. Committed to transforming conflict, Tectonic Leaders use the tension to inform themselves about the fears and transgenerational induced tensions that separate people in conflict.

3. Tectonic leaders lead consciously through the lens of evolution and not through the lens of survival

The paradox of survival is ultimately self-destructive. Survival resides in subconscious fear and the instinct to protect. While self-protection is "common sense," it is rooted in holding on to the footprint of the past. The evolutionary mindset, on the other hand, goes "beyond common sense." It is fueled by creativity, driven by a higher level of consciousness, and found in hope, posterity and a willingness to walk a path where there are no footprints.

These three disciplines and commitments of Tectonic Leadership are the guiding principles of all Tectonic Leadership processes and programs and the marching order for all Tectonic Leaders.

TECTONIC LEADERSHIP EXERCISE

Are you willing to care about others as much as you care about yourself?

Are you willing to develop a new relationship with tension—seeing tension as an opportunity to connect and not separate?

Are you willing to walk a path where there are no footprints? What could you create that will make a difference?

_____

_____

_____

_____

_____

_____

_____

_____

Harnessing the Power of Tension In Communities

If we don't learn to live together in mutual respect, then we are condemned to mutual destruction.

Rabbi David Rosen

"We Stand Together for Peace in Face of War" is an article that appeared in *The Muslim Observer* in 2012. Tectonic Leaders Lara Khadr, who has a master's degree from the University of Michigan School of Public Health in Hospital and Molecular Epidemiology, and Shahar Ben-Josef, who is a J.D./M.A. candidate in dispute resolution at Wayne State University in Detroit, Michigan, initiated the following article with contributing Tectonic Leaders Sarah Jaward, Jeff Lockwood, Abbeygail Epelman, Jacob Smith, John McDowell, Rachel Kaminsky, Brian Merlos, Rashid Beydoun, Hamzah Latif, Molly Manly, Ariana Segal.

As young Americans—Arab and Israeli, Christian, Jewish and Muslim— who are concerned and committed to transforming the all-encompassing Arab-Jewish conflict, our feelings of helplessness associated with current events in Israel-Palestine is overwhelming. Our feelings of guilt, shame, and utter horror boil beneath the surface as news and social media buzz with updates about death tolls and stances taken by world leaders. We are young adults who want to walk a path where there are no footprints. As graduates of the Tectonic Leadership Program, we seek to alter the course of human interactions by introducing people to new ways to dialogue effectively across dividing lines. Our relationships are built on the idea of allyhood. As Tectonic Leaders, we strive to care about the other as much as we care about our own, and we seek to utilize tension to find new solutions by developing deeper understandings of ourselves each other.

The escalation of violence in Israel and Gaza in the past week is part of a seemingly never-ending cycle that apparently, we should be accustomed to. We must ask: what is achieved through violence? The deaths of innocent civilians, whether they be Israeli or Palestinian, Jewish, Christian, or Muslim, will not lead the politicians to concede, nor will it in any way change the status quo. One of the greatest barriers to transforming the Arab-Israeli conflict is paranoia; there is a multitude of Israeli and Palestinian civilians who live in fear and are being conditioned to hate each and every day.

At first glance, it seems obvious and easy to blame the politicians for the war that they have started. But we must remember that we elected these politicians, we gave them our trust and our support, and it is up to us to tell them that we do not support these actions. It is easy to argue that while innocent Israelis and Palestinians pay the price of the uptake in violence, the politicians continue to define their strength by their willingness to protect their people by launching attacks on the other and by promulgating hate. Easier still to believe that politicians focus only on maintaining the survival of their people, but not on evolution and progression to ameliorate their people's well-being. We must ask our politicians to be truly strong and courageous, to face peace negotiations with open hearts and open minds, and with a willingness to make real compromise by caring equally for the social, political, and economic welfare of the other as much as they do for themselves.

Now is the time for us to change this thinking that has dominated the discourse surrounding the Arab-Jewish and Israeli-Palestinian conflicts for decades. Blaming politicians and *justifying or legitimizing acts of violence is an automatic response. No one wants to think that their people did anything wrong, and everyone views their own as the true victim. The common man feels powerless. But it is time to move past this way of thinking. While there is great power in advocating for one side or the other and it may seem intuitive to do so, there is also great limitation in focusing all of one's energies and attention on who is right and who is wrong. In order to move forward, we must look past our differences and embrace our common humanity.*

Together, as Tectonic Leaders, we recognize the horrendous impact of persistent rocket attacks and grueling air strikes, because those who bear the brunt of the violence, death, and destruction, are innocent. As Arabs, Israelis, Jews, Muslims, Christians, Americans, and most importantly, as human beings, we call for an immediate end to this round of violence. Together, we can create change, and now, more than ever, we must stand together.

Standing for peace in a time of war is the only true test of courage. We stand for peace. We ask you to join us.

Using Tension to Create Tectonic Shifts

You don't have to be wrong for me to be right.
**Brenda Rosenberg's "Reuniting the Children of Abraham:
A Toolkit 4 Peace"**

Teen's Mantra

For Brenda and many Jews, the fear of total annihilation spans 4,000 years of Jewish history. Not one generation has escaped that fear. What has been most unnerving for Jews is their ability to rise to greatness only to be persecuted and held in captivity. They are forced to bear witness to destruction of holy sites. They experience slavery and debasement. They are expelled and become victims to pogroms.

Six million Jews were dehumanized and murdered in the Holocaust, just because they were Jews. Wars between Arabs and Jews in 1948, 1967 and 1973 intensified the fear. Add to this the ongoing struggle not only to be recognized as a people in their historic Jewish homeland, but realizing that the world not acknowledge the expulsion of over 700,000 Jews from Arab countries at the time Israel was created. Past fears were reinforced by the second intifada, unending suicide bombings, rockets from Gaza and rants from Ahmadinejad calling for the destruction of Israel as Iran develops nuclear weapons.

Palestinians did not have their *an-Nakba* ("Day of the Catastrophe") officially recognized. During the *Nakba*, between 650,000 and 750,000 Palestinians were expelled from or fled from their homes in the midst of the creation of the state of Israel. People were deprived of realizing their dream to return to their homes, homes they are still holding the keys and deeds to. This number has grown to over 4.6 million displaced people.

About 3.7 million who are currently registered as refugees live in conditions of abject poverty. They, too, have experienced the humiliation of being occupied in their homeland, massacred at Deir Yassin and Shatila and never having received sufficient aid. They were not invited to assume citizenship in any neighboring country other than Jordan, and now even Jordan is limiting citizenship. They have been politically exploited by other Arabs and have had the legitimacy of their identities questioned and even denied. Those who have become Israeli citizens feel they are treated as second class, with travel restrictions and unequal rights. Tensions rise in revulsion as new settlements are authorized, leaving Palestinians feeling more oppressed by a continuing occupation. Those with a dual citizenship have to make a decision to return permanently or lose their homes.

Tectonic Leadership harnesses tensions as large as this Palestinian and Israeli conflict and uses that tension to build a new solution that not only satisfies both groups, but doesn't sacrifice either's identity or traditions. The following stories capture the essence of tectonic leadership in action.

From the Red Sea to the Mississippi

War does not determine who is right. Only who is left.

Bertrand Russell

Every tension has two truths

Brenda Rosenberg in Amman, Jordan

Thermometers pushed past 100 degrees. Smog and sand thickened the air. Even the pavement seemed to be on fire as I arrived in Amman, Jordan in July 2011 for an international conference on "Transforming Conflict: Sharing Tools for Cross-Cultural Dialogue." This was not my first visit to Jordan. I had been the guest of the royal family to participate in a global Abrahamic dialogue three years before. I arrived optimistic and confident, eager to present the Tectonic Leadership program.

I was looking forward to working with my friend Father Nabil Haddad who heads the Jordanian Interfaith Coexistence Research Center. I was also excited to meet and interact with new friends from Israel, the Palestinian territories, Jordan and Lebanon, who would be sharing their successful models for transforming conflict and creating cross-cultural understanding. I approached the podium wrapped with the red and white *keffiyeh*, a symbol of Jordanian heritage that Father Nabil Haddad had given me when he visited me at my home in Detroit. I was starry-eyed and exuberant as Father Haddad introduced me at the opening ceremony.

Then the microphone was handed to a man who said: "Hi, I'm Gadi from Tel Aviv." Next, there was an Arabic scream as a young man ran out of the room. Twenty young men and women followed him as two young women tugged on his jacket to pull him back into the room. I froze. My optimism vanished. All I could hear were echoes of my well-meaning friends and family: "Brenda, don't go!" "Jordan isn't safe!" Then, one of the organizers of the conference told me: "Brenda, protesters are out front. We have a bus at the side of the building for you and the Israelis. Leave now!" I walked to the bus, heart pounding, palms sweating. Who were these angry people? Why were they so furious?

Tanya Ghorra arrived the same day. She, too, was invited to attend the conference to lead a workshop on nonviolent communication. Fluent in Arabic, English and French, she served as the conference translator. Even though she came from the neighboring country of Lebanon, this was Tanya's first visit to Jordan. Growing up in Lebanon, she lived through many of the wars that devastated her tiny country.

In an article she published after the conference, entitled "When My Humanity and My Education Took Over My Reticence," Tanya wrote a heartwarming account of her experiences:

> *Having a Muslim mother and a Christian father did not help during those days. … I witnessed atrocities, lost friends and family, as many of us here did. I lost a childhood running from shelter to shelter. I was the alien when Christians killed Muslims and Muslims did the same. I had to hide so many times. If it wasn't an internal war, it was external. Palestinians used our land, Israelis used our land, Syrians used our land—killing few thousands more each time. Everyone had a cause, everyone had martyrs, and the rest were only victims. We survived … until the next round, always.*

In the lobby, there were many faces, and no time to say hello to everybody. Surprisingly, my eyes found a woman ... the minute I saw her, I thought to myself: She is assertive, like me! She must have felt the same, because the second after, she came and shook my hand and said: "Hi, I'm Brenda Naomi Rosenberg, I'm Jewish and I come from the United States." My smile faded for a second. Here I was, face to face with a Jew. But I said to myself, she's not an 'enemy' because she lives in the States. And I happen to have Jewish friends in Lebanon (they have always been here as Lebanese like me). We engaged in an exciting discussion. This woman is definitely the kind I like!

Once in the conference hall, I saw a woman, smiling at me. I smiled back. She looked very Lebanese to me. Oh, I thought I was the only one from Lebanon, but guess there's another Lebanese here, I thought to myself. She approached me with emotion in her eyes. She asked me if I was Lebanese. I replied with a big smile and the same inquiry. The most amazing thing happened. With tears in her eyes, she said, "I have something to tell you, and when I'm done, I want to kiss your cheeks and give you a big hug."

She told me that she came to this conference hoping to meet someone from Lebanon. She's a Lebanese Jew. She left Lebanon when she was 15 and traveled to France and the United States before settling in Tel Aviv. Now she's a peace activist. I was overwhelmed.

I wracked my brain: She is Lebanese, but she is an Israeli citizen. OK, she is here because she is a peace activist, but come on, she represents a country that occupied my land for years with the world watching! OK, we have too much in common, with the same memories and pain, same language. But, she chose to be on the other side! And what? She comes with a whole big group of Israelis too?

What am I going to do? Where did I put myself? My people suffered. Lives and properties lost can never be forgotten. We still have all the Palestinian refugees because of them! We were the only Arab country to pay the bloodiest price for the Palestinian-Israeli conflict! My country is still at war with them! 2006 is not history.

I will be in deep trouble with my country when I go back! I can be sentenced to jail and who knows if not capital punishment in case they know I spoke to these people! I can be accused of treason.

But while having all these thoughts in my head, my heart pushed me to hold Frida, a Jew from Tel Aviv, very close. We both cried.

--

Those four days went so quickly. But a huge human experience occurred. And it changed my life. I discovered Israelis and Palestinians working to build bridges across madness, hand in hand. I discovered peace builders. I discovered beautiful souls. Throughout these days, I was able to discuss my country's point of view and listen to their point of view. I was able to say face to face what seemed non-feasible a week before. I had the chance to play the interpreter in many workshops and sessions. While there, I translated so many opposing feelings,

Frida and Tanya

pain, oppression, hurt, anger, and deceit. I had to be faithful to all these feelings, even when they were far from my beliefs. I had to have big ears, big eyes and a big heart to capture everything and translate. That exercise forced me to be deeply human. It forced me to take every feeling and live it. And that wasn't so hard. In fact, I found myself in every story and every negative or positive feeling. I came back home more human. Now I have faces and names for the "others."

When the microphone was handed Gadi from Tel Aviv, the next thing I heard was a man screaming in Arabic. Tanya, on

From left to right: Sarah Jaward, an Arab American and a graduate of the Tectonic Leadership program, Brenda Rosenberg and Tanya Ghorra at the Transforming Conflict Conference in Amman, Jordan (2011)

the other hand, heard something very different. She writes, "The clash that occurred in everyone's presence helped me a lot. A group of Jordanian-Palestinian participants rushed outside and became angry with the Israeli presence. They said organizers didn't mention it, and they threatened to leave the conference. It was good to know I wasn't the only one having thoughts about the issue.

But I wasn't going to do the same thing. That's just not me. I looked into the Israeli participants' faces and felt empathy. I wouldn't want to be in their shoes! And so I don't want to act aggressively! We're here to engage in a multicultural dialogue to better transform conflict, remember?"

What frightened me and nearly sent me back home is what comforted Tanya and kept her in the conference.

As our discussions deepened, we saw the barriers to peace are greater than land and maps, language, and religion.

We recognized our own trans-generational wounding—the pain we carry consciously and unconsciously from past and current experience—both personally and collectively.

Learning from those truths

Coming from opposite sides of the fault line, these two peace activists, who traveled long distances at their own expense to transform conflict, found themselves in the same situation with a very different experience of the incident. Despite the difficulty of the situation, they both made the decision to stay. Their barriers were broken, their fears transformed, their lives changed. They used tension to deepen their understanding of the other and created a sustainable friendship without giving up their core beliefs.

"Don't be afraid to stick your neck out. Be like giraffes and have each other's backs."
Tanya Ghorra

Jewish and Arab Children of Haifa
turned a divide into a work of art.

Another Disruptive Departure

Brenda Rosenberg in Jordan

As I was presenting the Tectonic Leadership model, a young Palestinian man left the room. At lunch, Osama, the Palestinian who bolted from the presentation, asked if we could talk. He explained that he left the session because he was overcome with emotion and didn't want anyone to see him shed a tear. He wanted to learn more about our programs. He was touched to see a Jew from America care so deeply about both Israelis and Palestinians.

"The enemy is fear. We think it's hate, but it is fear."
Gandhi
Found on Osama's Facebook page

I assumed this young man left the session in a show of anger over something I said—yet here we were hugging and snapping photos and promising to stay in touch.

And we did. I visited Osama in the West Bank two years later, and we keep in touch on Facebook.

TV TECTONIC LEADERSHIP EXERCISE

In what you have read so far, what surprised you? What moved you? What troubled you?

_____

_____

_____

_____

_____

_____

_____

_____

_____

Leading Tectonically

"Negotiation is not a matter of give and take. Every solution that exists is dead. If you have two solutions, don't waste the time in trying to convince the other party about your solution. Try to create a third solution, which is unknown."

Shimon Peres

As Brenda and Samia shared more stories, they realized how much Jewish fear and Arab anger permeated their communities. Brenda was exposed at a very young age to horrific images of the Holocaust and the Jewish history of persecution. Even though she has not lost a single relative in the Holocaust or any war, she shares a real fear of annihilation with other Jews. Samia's loss of a grandmother and great aunt, burned to death by Israeli raids on Southern Lebanon in 1982, and the displacement of her family during the 2006 war added to the rage she felt when she visited Palestinians refugee camps in Lebanon. Her anger towards Israelis intensified as she demonized all Jews trying to justify Israel's actions. Brenda and Samia both saw how important it was to hear each other's stories and to know how both Jews and Arabs saw themselves as victims and perceived the other as the terrorist.

It was the presence, not the absence, of tension that deepened Samia and Brenda's relationship. While they were brought together by a common teacher and shared values of justice, it is their differences and the power of the tension that kept them together and fueled their commitment and obsession to collaborate and co-create a shared vision despite their polarized beliefs. This was the basis upon which Tectonic Leadership was created.

Harnessing the Power of Tension between Police and Community

True peace is not merely the absence of tension, it is the presence of justice.

Martin Luther King Jr.

Story by Brenda Naomi Rosenberg

February 14, 2015. It was a very gloomy Valentine's Day. My heart was heavy with sadness. Tears welled in my eyes as I walked into the memorial service for Dan Krichbaum. Dan was a powerful and relentless force for justice, a champion of bringing communities together. Many fond memories came to mind as I made my way down the aisle at the Birmingham Methodist Church in Birmingham, Michigan.

Dan was a great supporter of my interfaith efforts. He recruited me as the first female member for the board of MRDI (Michigan Roundtable for Diversity and Inclusion) Interfaith Partners. Dan helped bring my project, "Reuniting the Children of Abraham: A Toolkit 4 Peace," to congregations, and he honored me with the Michigan Roundtable for Diversity and Inclusion (MRDI) Community Service Award.

As I neared the front, I spotted Steve Spreitzer, president and CEO of the Michigan Roundtable for Diversity and Inclusion, and sat next to him. We shared humorous and anguished memories of working with Dan, our sadness of his passing and our concerns of the deepening fault lines between the police and community throughout the U.S.

Steve invited me to attend the next meeting of ALPACT (Advocates and Leaders for Police and Community Trust) meeting. ALPACT was looking for programs to combat the hate and tension between the police force and southeastern Michigan communities, and he thought Tectonic Leadership could be utilized. I attended the meeting in Dearborn, Michigan and listened to the tensions that both community and law enforcement voiced. ALPACT co chair Heidi Budaj, executive director of the Michigan Anti Defamation League put me on the agenda for the next meeting in New Baltimore, Michigan. I wrote down every word of the feelings and tensions expressed in that room:

COMMUNITY

they feel

unheard
disrespected
lorded over
harassed
black discrimination
distrust of police
frustrated from lack of progress
provoked
police need better training
need for police psychological evaluations

POLICE

they feel

hated
verbally abused
disrespected
constantly pitted against citizens
misunderstood
they put their lives in danger to provide order
they are the safety net and 911 link
they enforce justice
can't recruit minorities

I explained how this was the starting point of Tectonic Leadership's four-step process (see appendix). Exceptional enthusiasm filled the room. Both community and law enforcement saw the possibilities. They were willing to address the tension that was dividing them. They saw the power in harnessing the tension—and by addressing the tension they saw the possibility to build alliances across the divide. I left the meeting elated. I received no formal handshake, only hugs.

I began meeting with police chiefs, community leaders, religious leaders and educators. Currently, we are finalizing the "Future Tectonic Leaders Tool Kit" with Roseville, Michigan—a program, documentary, and set of educational materials to bridge the divide between police and community—to act as a model for every community in America. Below is the executive summary.

Future Tectonic Leaders

Objective

To bridge the disconnect between community and law enforcement by informing, engaging and empowering students to become problem solvers. Furthermore, working with police to find a solution together for their community through 10 weekly meetings.

Goals

Students will be informed and educated through Tectonic Leadership by experiencing first hand:

Texting-while-driving simulator

Drunk driving simulator

F.A.T.S. (Firearms training system)

Watching films of real life experiences of encounters between police and lawbreakers, then role-playing the experience

How to respond to situations with police (i.e. being pulled over, riot breaking out at a football game, becoming a victim of cyberbullying)

Training in diversity awareness, cultural competency, and leadership skills to bridge divides through programming (provided by Tectonic Leadership Center, Anti-Defamation League (ADL), No Place

for Hate and the Michigan Round Table for Diversity
and Inclusion Cultural Competency Program)

Engaging in the creative arts and social media as a tool
for social expression and healing

Providing leadership and conflict transformation skills
for use at home, at school, at work, in the community
and in the world

Learning about potential internships and opportunities
in the field of law enforcement

OUTCOME

Ultimately, the Tectonic Leadership model will create sustainable solutions for bridging the disconnect between law enforcement and students through:

Deconstructing negative images of law enforcement and
its relationship with disenfranchised members of the
community

Teaching young student leaders the skills necessary
to transform the tension between police and
community with the knowledge that addressing both
sides' needs does not equate to a zero-sum game

Empowering students so that they can make a
difference—creating justice is in their hands.

Sharing a "Future Tectonic Leaders" program via a
documentary and educational toolkit

Looking back at my conversation with Steve, I can't help but think of my dear friend Suzy Farbman, who wrote a wonderful book called *God Signs*. Suzy inspires me to continually watch for signs of guidance from God—signs of hope and infinite possibilities. I can't help but think that reconnecting with Steve Spritzer at Dan Krichbaum's memorial service was a sign from God. Dan is our peace angel.

Harnessing the Power of Tension Across Divides

One University of Michigan-Dearborn student's involvement in leadership programs leads to having compassion for both sides of the Middle East conflict.

Story by Abbeygail Omaits, 2013 University of Michigan-Dearborn graduate and current bioarchaeologist, published in the September 8, 2011 edition of the Detroit-Jewish News.

What if you went through your entire life and one day you reflect back and realize you had never traveled to that one place of your dreams? You ponder on the experience, why you want it so badly, what you would gain from going there, and then you have a choice.

Do you commit to the idea and start to research, plan and act? Or do you shrug off the idea as a good yet unobtainable dream? Perhaps you leave it to faith to allow it to happen in your lifetime, but it's not for you to initiate? This same process goes through our minds when it comes to peace and especially action needed to obtain peace in the Middle East.

So, why is it that such a good idea, an idea like peace, isn't embraced and acted upon by all? Is it because not all feel they are capable of such an endeavor? Or perhaps they don't have the drive for a better tomorrow? Or maybe they feel like someone else will take care of it.

Peace and coexistence take every single person to achieve. We need to eliminate the mindset that "one day someone else will do it."

Because that one day is today, and the someone is us.

I started my undergraduate degree at the University of Michigan-Dearborn in the fall of 2009. It was the first time I had been introduced to such a large Arab American population and, being an anthropology major with a minor in religious studies, I was pretty excited to learn and observe a population unfamiliar to me. I made friends with many men and women in my classes; I asked a ton of questions and even read the Koran.

Minor incidents started occurring on campus that made me less comfortable with my Jewish identity. There were many anti-Zionist and anti-Israel organizations on campus and, to me, that meant anti-Jewish. Such incidents and misunderstandings lead me to not wear my Star of David to school. I didn't involve myself much with the Jewish community or speak up because I didn't want my social life negatively affected.

My second year at UM-D, I decided I wouldn't put up with the one-sided promotions any more. I have always been an outspoken woman, and this year it really came out. Organizations like ASU (Arab Student Union), MSA (Muslim Student Association), HOPE (Humanitarian Organization for Palestinian Equality) had events year-round involving anti-Israel topics. I made an effort to get the materials they were passing out, and I was shocked – could these statistics and facts be correct? Maybe Israel isn't what I thought it was after all?

My doubt concerned me; I stuck up for Israel whenever I had the chance to, but what was I suppose to say when the things I read left me speechless? I was one person. I was outnumbered, and I didn't know where to start. I saw an announcement on the Hillel of Metro Detroit website for a fellowship involving Israel advocacy and I submitted my resume.

I was accepted into the fellowship, which lasted 10 weeks and covered a variety of topics such as the history, military, lifestyles, conflict, international industry and Israel right here in

Michigan. The fellowship not only strengthened my identity as a Jew, but also as a Zionist, a member of the community and an advocate for the positive outcomes of the Jewish State of Israel.

New Type Of Leadership

During one of our sessions, I was introduced to Brenda Rosenberg, who spoke to me about a pilot leadership program called Tectonic Leadership. I was immediately interested. She called, and I was admitted into the five-day retreat in early May.

The days leading up to the retreat were uneasy. I had no idea what to expect or how to behave. The only people I knew going into the retreat were my good friends Hussein Berry and Hamzah Latif, both are Muslim students at UM-D.

The retreat was held at the Manresa Jesuit Retreat House in Bloomfield Hills and opened on Yom HaShoah, a day I hold close to my heart, being a firstgeneration Holocaust survivor's decedent. Normally, I spend the day in quiet meditation, reflecting on my life, and those of my grandparents, great grandparents and family affected by the Holocaust, hoping that their struggles make me a stronger person. Brenda spoke beautifully about the importance of Yom HaShoah and lit a candle in memory of all the lives lost. As tears fell from my eyes, Hussein squeezed my hand and I knew from that moment on that this would be a life-changing week.

Throughout the days of the Tectonic Leadership retreat, 15 other Muslim, Jewish and Christian students and I learned the disciplines and commitments of Tectonic Leadership. We created bonds with each other that no one could replace. We shared our pain, positive experiences, tears, frustration, happiness and most of all, a common goal for peaceful solutions.

Samia Bahsoun and Brenda Rosenberg, creators of Tectonic Leadership, inspired, challenged and motivated us continuously with their wisdom and experience in conflict resolution and the beautiful friendship they have created. Throughout the week, not only did I learn so much from the Muslim perspective, but also I stopped seeing them as "the other" and began seeing them as my brothers and sisters. I looked around the room and did not see individuals, but all of us as one, working together to see tension as an opportunity, not an obstacle in partnering.

A surprising thing happened during my time at Manresa: My core beliefs about Israel and my Jewish and Zionist identity strengthened as did my understanding of the Palestinian pain.

I realized that you do not have to give up any of your beliefs to accept another's. One doesn't have to be wrong, so another can be right.

The lines and differences between Palestine and Israel have faded. The people are one, brothers and sisters. There is nothing more important than saving human lives. The world is full of people who want to be better, different and superior. Every single human being means just as much as the next, and one life is as important as your own; neither of you are replaceable.

Tectonic Leadership was a life-changing experience, and one that will continue throughout my life. We are committed to a friendship and unbreakable bond with each other. We are committed to bringing peace and understanding to all that we can reach.

The Holocaust

A Continuing Point of Tension

It was the second morning of a 5-day Tectonic Leadership pilot workshop on the conflict in the Middle East. Brenda and Samia drove the short distance from Brenda's home to Manresa Jesuit Retreat Center, both located in Bloomfield Hills, Michigan. They joined 16 student leaders from five universities in Michigan who were laughing and sharing breakfast.

It seemed the paradoxical approach seemed to have created bonds from day one of the workshop. The participants thought they would start slow and spend the first days getting acquainted. But, Brenda and Samia felt it was critical to create a situation of tension that would expose the issues surrounding conflict between the students. Suicide bombings were at the top of the list.

On day one of the workshop, students watched the documentary *To Die in Jerusalem*, a movie that tells the story of two Jewish mothers searching for answers to the deaths of their daughters. One mother wanted to know why her daughter, a 17-year-old Arab honors student who was engaged to married, had killed herself and many others in a suicide bombing in Jerusalem. The other mother hardly found a moment of peace after her 17-year-old daughter was killed by the same teenage suicide bomber. When the families tried to put the body parts together for burial, they couldn't tell the two girls' limbs apart.

The students couldn't look away, shedding tears as they followed the encounters of the two mothers. Every interaction and conversation was disastrous—both mothers were disrespectful. Neither listened, and they constantly challenged each other. There was no attempt to engage and find an understanding that both mothers were looking for. The documentary ends with feelings of complete hopelessness—most viewers would leave the movie thinking it is impossible for any Israeli and Arab to talk to each other, let alone create peace. Yet for the students, the debriefing turned out to be an eye- and heart-opener.

The Arab students heard the Jewish students express their shame at how the Jewish mother treated the Arab mother and the Jewish students heard the Arab students' fury when the Arab mother didn't respond to the Jewish mother. After the debriefing, the students spent the remainder of the afternoon in tectonic role-playing:

1. *What could have changed if the mothers had utilized the tension of this horrific event instead of it using them?*

2. *How would their conversation have changed if they had taken the Tectonic pledge to care about the other as much as you care about yourself?*

3. *What if they paired?*

4. *What could they have said to both communities? What could they have done together that would help both communities?*

The role-playing and visioning of what could be gave them hope. They saw that they could partner with someone who they perceived as a stranger (or even an enemy) just hours before.

Tension is seldom eradicated

The second day's morning session began with talking about *Yom Ha Shoah*, or Holocaust Remembrance Day. Brenda shared the story of Ahmadinejad's raging denial of the Holocaust at the 2009 U.N. meeting in Geneva. Teri, a Lebanese American participant, raised her OUCH! card. (The 4" x 6" card was emblazoned with the word "OUCH!" in red letters. It gave participants a way of signaling that they heard a word or concept that troubled them. It's an effective tool because participants' reactions were immediately acknowledged without interrupting the speaker.)

After the speaker finished, Teri shared her OUCH!: "You have to take the Holocaust off the table. If you don't I am leaving the workshop." Brenda was stunned. She stood and announced she was not taking the Holocaust off the table. Terry gathered up her things and walked out.

Steve Olewan, a Muslim psychologist, spend the next few hours listening, talking and wiping Teri's tears. When the group broke for lunch, Samia and Brenda went to talk with Teri. The team recognized that the Holocaust was why they began their work together. They knew as Jews and Arabs that it would always be a point of tension. They knew they had two very different truths. Teri was outraged that Brenda, as a Jew, needed Muslims and Arabs to speak out against Ahmadinejad's Holocaust denial remarks. What was common sense for Brenda made no sense to Teri.

Brenda was unable to have Teri agree with her, no matter what. The tension of the Holocaust was using them. Samia and Brenda went back to their mantra, *"How can we use the tension surrounding the Holocaust instead of it using us?"* and went back to the guiding force of the three disciplines and commitments of Tectonic Leadership:

How can we pair and use tension to create deeper understanding? How can we demonstrate our commitment to care

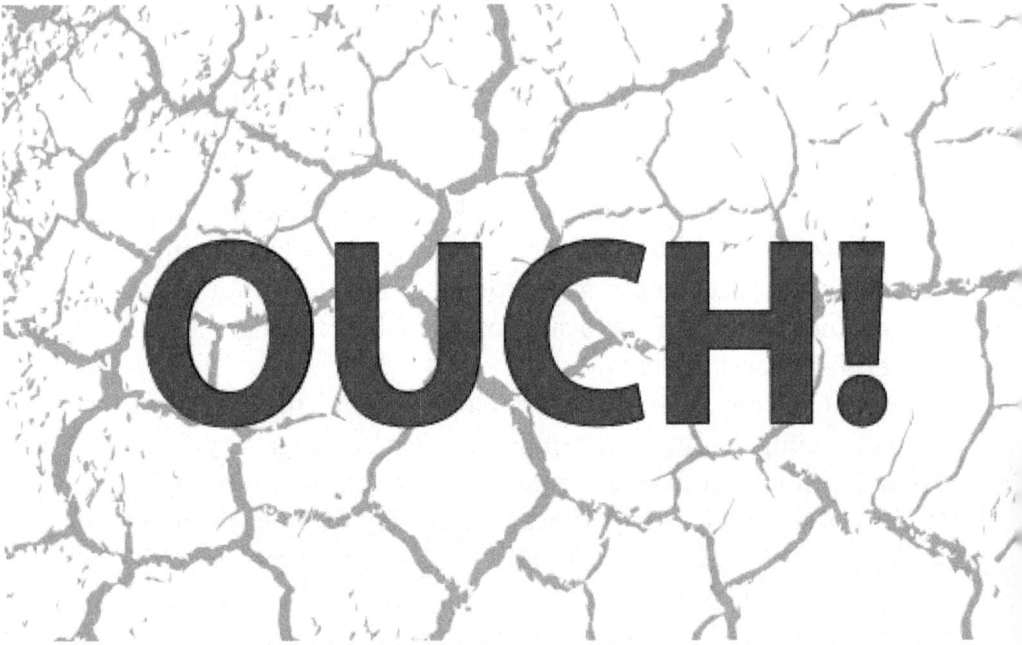
OUCH!

equally about self and other? How can we work together to help both our communities?

Brenda asked Teri what the most important issue for her was. She responded, the plight of the Palestinians. She asked if Teri would be willing to stay if they looked at both the plight of the Palestinians and the Holocaust together. She agreed. After lunch, the group role-played the tension. They went around the room alternating group designation as one or two. Group one was Holocaust survivors, and group two was Palestinian refugees. They used role-playing as an opportunity to deepen understanding of each other, connect at a deeper level and find new solutions together. Each group was assigned to answer the following questions:

1. What could you say to the other group to that would express your identity and pain and give voice to recognizing their identity and pain?
2. What could you say to the other group that would engage them, inspire them to work with you and bring a new level of understanding?
3. What could you say to the other group that would build trust and give them hope that together, as partners, it is possible to create a safe and just future for your communities and all of humanity?

The results were amazing. Within two hours, the groups came together and shared their responses to the three questions.

You can watch the video: "Using Tension to Transform Conflict" at: http://youtu.be/2Fr6yT5XVUI

Teri was randomly selected to be part of group one with Rashid Baydoun, a Muslim, Ariana Segal Mentzel, a Jewish Zionist and child of Holocaust survivor, and Jacob Smith, a Christian. Terry wanted to take the lead. These are the words from her group, Holocaust survivors, speaking to Palestinians:

We are your Christian brothers and sisters, have come here to Israel as survivors of the Holocaust in recognition of the pain of the Palestinian people.

We acknowledge that you, oh people of Gaza, feel imprisoned, as well as hopeless and despair. We too, as survivors of the Holocaust have also experienced this kind of pain.

As survivors of the Holocaust, we understand how death, destruction, and hate have poisoned our peoples and how this threat continues to plight us to this very day.

Instead of using our pain and trauma to further victimize one another, perpetuating the damage and destruction, we plead with you, oh people of Gaza. We humbly ask you to take our hands as we invite you into our hearts. We ask that you embark on this journey with us, the survivors of the Holocaust. We believe that as we share our pain, and our stories, our lives and our hearts; that we can find common good to end future hostilities, blockades and destruction; and that we can end further terror and trauma. We, the survivors of the Holocaust, embark to this new future with you, the people of Gaza. Just as we, the survivors of the Holocaust, seek protection and safety from future atrocities, we pledge our commitment to the people of Gaza to extend those same rights to you.

Let us work together to form a life time partnership for the welfare of our people's lives and for lives and future, for our Israeli and Palestinian children."

Teri not only went on to complete the Tectonic Leadership workshop, she went on to get an "A" in a Holocaust study program at the University of Michigan-Dearborn and continues to work with Tectonic Leadership today.

TECTONIC LEADERSHIP EXERCISE

Pick a situation of tension in your personal life or in your community and map it using the tectonic process:

Discovery: identify the elements of conflict and clearly articulate the real needs of people in conflict

Apply the three disciplines and commitment of Tectonic Leadership

_____

_____

_____

_____

_____

_____

_____

_____

_____

Harnessing the Power of Tension In Education

Tectonic Leadership in Practice with Students

Rashid Baydoun's story as told by Leslie Alter, University of Michigan student and 2015 Tectonic Leadership intern

After a past filled with tension, Rashid realized how to harness it for the betterment of a community.

"If a student can't read, we teach them how to read. If a student can't do math, we teach them how to do math. If a student can't do science, we teach them how to do science. If a student misbehaves, we punish them? Or do we teach them how to behave?"

This question is one that Restorative Justice/Practices Coordinator Rashid Baydoun is working to change the answer to at Stout Middle School in Dearborn, Michigan, his hometown. At the age of 29, this University of Michigan-Dearborn graduate "creates connections amongst the community, teachers and students alike, while providing much needed assistance and training with affective communication skills and interventions."

"Often time, students with broken households struggle and societal problems are pushed to the schools with little assistance to solve these problems. Problems a traditional teacher is not equipped to handle. I work alongside various mental health professions including social workers and various therapists in order to find the root of the problem and build connections. Our schools have become the front where we learn a lot about the communities we serve and for the most part, at school is where the diagnosis meets the various challenges."

While enrolled at the University of Michigan-Dearborn, Baydoun, a devout Muslim Arab, was the president of the Arab Civic Union and went on to be the advisor. At this point in his life, he describes his point of view as one-sided. An American-born citizen with parents from southern Lebanon and directly affected by the war in 1982, he started boycott divestment and sanctions against Israel on his campus.

Although Baydoun now describes himself as a "hot commodity" in the educational restorative justice movement, he shares that he wouldn't have seen himself in this line of work in 2011 when he went through Tectonic Leadership.

"I filled out the application [for Tectonic Leadership] just to appease [a friend]. I was trying not to be selected so I used inflammatory words to possibly cause people to look at it and think this person doesn't seem like they want to be constructive but rather deconstructive."

Despite the fact that Baydoun was not looking to change his point of view on the conflict in the Middle East, his one-sided perspective on the issue was exactly what Brenda and Samia were looking for in considering candidates for the program.

"I was very outspoken and very raw. I wasn't interested in making friends or making any type of connection and at first I really did not want to be there whatsoever. I was kind of frightened and intimidated that I was showing my vulnerability. And there I represented the Arab Civic Union which made me think I had to bring my A game everyday. I felt like I needed boxing gloves and thought it was about who can survive 12 rounds."

Baydoun attributes his success as a Restorative Justice/Practices Coordinator to Tectonic Leadership, claiming it allowed him to learn this restorative justice process.

"Once you learn that there's two sides to a voice you begin to understand that one needs to come to the table first and that's something I was unable to do prior to Tectonic Leadership. [It's an issue] getting people on the same page and getting them at the table, [but] if you're not at the table, you're on the menu. If anyone is not at the table, they will think we weren't part of the discussion so obviously they were the topic of discussion and then they don't feel valued or appreciated."

After going through Tectonic Leadership, Baydoun applies many of the same principles and strategies to his own conversation circles and interventions with much success, shown by the 30 percent drop in suspensions at Stout Middle School since he assumed this position.

"The reason I believe Tectonic Leadership works is because it's willing to use the actual tension and address the very harm and pain that an individual has. If you don't address the elephant in the room, if you don't address the actual pain, then all we are doing is masking it. We're putting a Band-Aid on this huge wound and the Band-Aid isn't big enough. We have to do something to actually repair that harm."

Baydoun sees the positive impact Tectonic Leadership has within his community, and hopes to see these tools and techniques used in more organizations.

"The missing link to many great programs in place is Tectonic Leadership and tectonic approaches and language and that's because it's messy. Emotions are messy and most of the time people want those closed in walls but ordinary people need to be equipped with the tools needed to communicate."

Sometimes, we all need a helping hand.

Our Tectonic Wish

"Imagination is the beginning of creation. You imagine what you desire, you will what you imagine and at last you create what you will."

George Bernard Shaw

Generating a Tectonic Movement

Imagine how the world would change if people from opposite sides of conflict used tension to create partnerships across the divides. What if Jews and Arabs, Shia and Sunni Muslims, Hutu and Tutsi, Republicans and Democrats paired to create viable and sustainable partnerships in business, government, policy-making, public service, the arts and science? These partnerships could benefit both communities that are currently in conflict.

The mission of Tectonic Leadership is to duplicate the unlikely partners Brenda and Samia have become as a result of using divisive tension to connect their communities.

Their objective is to deconstruct the myths, prejudices and stereotypes that deter partnerships across a new pool of young leaders from their religious, cultural, racial, political, and socio economic divides. Furthermore, Tectonic Leadership seeks to eliminate the entrenched belief "there is no partner on the other side."

Brenda and Samia are seeking a permanent home for the Tectonic Leadership Center in a university, law school or within a network of college campuses across the country. They seek a safe space for people from opposite sides of conflict to come together, deconstruct negative narratives and build a new joint narrative. In this space, leaders will develop trust in each other and commit to:

Lead together: While the traditional leadership model rewards individual leadership, Tectonic Leadership rewards leadership in pairs—pairs of opposite side of conflict leading together. Under this model, leaders commit to care equally for self and other. Paired Tectonic Leaders create paired communities—these communities and their constituents hold them accountable.

Use tension as a connector to bridge their differences and expand their boundaries: Tectonic Leadership revisits the role of tension in leadership and negotiation. Traditional negotiating techniques focus on commonalities and aim at compromise. Tectonic Leadership explores and addresses the points of tension and uses this information to bridge the divide.

Under traditional leadership approaches, people in conflict miss the opportunity to engage fully with the other, understand the other and verbalize their differences. Avoiding tension becomes a form of censorship. In the Tectonic Leadership approach, the premise is that tension is never eradicated. Tectonic Leaders harness tension to deconstruct the conflicting political, cultural, social and economic narratives and create partnerships across the divides that benefit both communities and build trust. In action, tension informs each side about the other and creates a new discourse.

Build social or business enterprises together: Tectonic Leadership bridges the economic divide with a social and business entrepreneurial platform that encourages participation and partnerships across the divides. The Tectonic Leadership model broadens the entrepreneurial spirit by pairing people on opposite sides of conflict to create prosperity for self while creating prosperity for the other, thus producing a level of "positive" interdependency that transcends conflict and benefits both communities.

Create policies together: Tectonic Leadership introduces a new form of governance, defined by inclusive policies created and implemented by representatives from communities in conflict, which respect and serve all communities and become the framework of a new relational architecture.

Construct a multimedia communication forum: Tectonic leaders build and maintain open forums for people on opposite sides of ethnic tension, border conflicts and economic disparity. These forums allow users to present their stories on how they paired across the divide, deconstructed their negative narratives, developed trust, partnered and stayed committed to each other.

To practice Tectonic Leadership and observe other video/ technological resources that put Tectonic Leadership into action, visit the "Practicing Tectonic Leadership" and "Resources" appendices at the end of this book.

Practicing Tectonic Leadership

Your guide to harnessing the power of tension to build alliances in your life

STEP 1 – Name the tension that is dividing you

Example: Disconnect between community and law enforcement

STEP 2 – Describe the tension on each side

All parties in conflict are given permission to clearly express their feelings surrounding the situation of tension without feeling criticized or censored.

Exercise:

1. Describe the situation of tension
2. Name your feelings: angry, hurt, disappointed, frustrated, helpless, hopeless, uncomfortable, impatient, overwhelmed, etc.

Example:

Community tension: feel unheard, disrespected, lorded over, harassed, and bias against blacks, do not trust police, frustrated nothing will be done, police provoke anger, feel police need better training and psychological evaluations

Law enforcement tension: everyone hates us, spits on us, no respect, feel it is always us vs them, feel misunderstood - we put our lives in danger to provide order, we are the safety net, the 911link, we enforce justice. We can't recruit minorities.

STEP 3 – Bridge the divide by harnessing the power of tension

The intent is develop a new relationship with tension by:

Understanding that Tension will never be eradicated

Expanding boundaries without changing core beliefs, knowing that one can validate the feelings of the other without agreeing with the other

Harnessing the power of Tension to connect and not separate, utilizing tension as an opportunity to deconstruct negative narratives, deepen understanding and not as an obstacle in partnering

Exercise:

1. What could you say to the other to express your position and your pain?
2. How can you respond to the other recognizing their position and pain?
3. What could you say to the other that would engage them, inspire them to work with you and bring a new level of understanding?
4. What could you say to the other that would build trust, and give them hope that together as partners it is possible to create a safe and just future for your communities and all of humanity?

STEP 4 – Lead tectonically by harnessing the power of tension

Partner with someone from the opposite side of conflict. Tectonic partners holding each other accountable to stay committed to the relationship, especially during times of crisis.

Tectonic partners willingly stand with each other and engage both communities - actualizing a shared congruent identity without changing core beliefs.

Concrete Action Steps:

1. Find a partner on the other side and commit together to the disciplines and commitments of Tectonic Leadership
2. Together create a project that would benefit both parties knowing that each party might have different needs
3. Create a plan that includes:
   a. Your vision, goals and milestones
   b. A list of obstacles you foresee and the resources you might need to mitigate them
   c. A support structure to assure sustainability

Resources

Duel historic narrative of Middle East conflict www.vispo.com/PRIME

Common Ground News—published weekly—constructive articles that foster dialogue on global conflicts www.commongroundnews.org

From Enemies to Tectonic Leaders: Samia Moustapha Bahsoun & Brenda Naomi Rosenberg http://youtu.be/UtsOlXeRfT4

How Brenda & Samia utilized the tension surrounding the Holocaust to deepen their understanding of each others beliefs—inspiring the unlikely pair to create The Tectonic Leadership Center for Conflict Transformation and Cross Cultural Communication. Their goal—prevent future genocides.

Tectonic Leadership Center for Conflict Transformation and Cross Cultural Communication http://youtu.be/6YQCIIZjpnA

A new way of leading—a new way of living. The Tectonic Leadership Center develops and trains existing leaders and potential leaders from opposite sides of conflict to take joint ownership in transforming conflict, facing challenges together and finding solutions together.

Using TENSION to transform conflict http://youtu.be/2Fr6yT5XVUI

The Tectonic Leadership Center demonstrates how, by role-playing the "enemy," participants can utilize tension as an opportunity to transform relationships, build trust, and create solutions together.

Rashid Baydoun, Tectonic Leader http://youtu.be/
B95t5CQAL2g

Meet Rashid as he shares his experiences at the
Tectonic Leadership Retreat for Middle East Conflict
Transformation.

Reuniting the Children of Abraham http://youtu.
be/294XNY8EnWU

A multimedia tool kit 4 peace—creating a new level of
understanding between faiths and cultures

**The Council for a Parliament of World Religions
Webinar Faiths against Hate:** Tectonic Leadership
from Conflict Transformation and Cross Cultural
Communication http://www.youtube.com/
watch?v=9JfH2P10nsg

**Tectonic Leadership presentation at the Holocaust
Memorial Center** in conjunction with BESA—
Albanian Muslims who rescued Jews during the
Holocaust http://youtu.be/0Hb0Viv9Pj8

My Jewish Detroit http://myjewishdetroit.org/2014/11/
tectonic-leadership/

Front page of Jewish Forward http://bit.ly/1MG95TU

CPSIA information can be obtained
at www.ICGtesting.com
Printed in the USA
LVOW02s0949200916

505292LV00002B/2/P